Confessions of

a

Limousine

Chauffeur

Carmen V. Stern

authorHOUSE®

AuthorHouse™
1663 Liberty Drive
Bloomington, IN 47403
www.authorhouse.com
Phone: 1-800-839-8640

First published by AuthorHouse   06/21/2011

ISBN: 978-1-4634-2811-2 (sc)
ISBN: 978-1-4634-2810-5 (ebk)

Printed in the United States of America

Any people depicted in stock imagery provided by Thinkstock are models, and such images are being used for illustrative purposes only.
Certain stock imagery © Thinkstock.

This book is printed on acid-free paper.

INTRODUCTION

I can think of a hundred different times, dates and occasions when I would have liked to be surprised with a limousine. On my 30th birthday ... on my 40th birthday... when I became a grandmother... or how about just a good special occasion!

I love my husband dearly, but his timing for gifts is awful. I had just gotten a new job working as a Spanish teacher in a private school and on the second day of school I came down with the worst flu. It was flu season in November. This bout with the flu lasted me 7 weeks; 3 of which I was in bed, flat on my back. It was the 3rd week of my flu that I got this great surprise. Any other time I would have been running and jumping, but it was all I could do to create energy for myself to sit up in bed!

At first; when I got the news, I thought my husband was just kidding with me to get me to look lively again, but I knew it was for real when he told me we needed to drive to Tacoma to pick it up from the seller. I knew that he would not have me drive to Tacoma as poorly as I was feeling with my bones feeling like cracked ice. But it was for real and so off we went.

We arrived and the car was just beautiful and classic. It was just a dream car. This was a 1989 Lincoln 105 inch stretch limousine, with burgundy velvet seats. The body was in wonderful condition but looking like it needed a woman's touch. My husband had bought it for $6,000.00 and for what we could see it looked like it was well worth it. The seller told me that this car had come from Beverly Hills and I could see that by the tag on the metal. He also told me that John Candy (now deceased) was a frequent client of this car as also Bob Hope and Sophia Loren had been a couple of times.

After my husband finalized the paperwork and the keys were in my hand I began to be a little nervous about driving such a long car home, but I reminded myself that I have driven a 26 foot long U-haul up the side of a mountain in snow, at night. If I could do that, I could certainly get this limo home on the freeway. And I did. It was a little scary but I would soon be backing this long long car down my driveway as if I had been doing it all my life.

While driving home, I thought to myself "so what exactly are the things I can do with this car?"

The realities were about to begin….

CHAPTER ONE

It's the Autumn of 1999.

I work three jobs. I get up at 6 a.m. and by 7 a.m. I'm in Seattle to take care of a senior lady getting her up and dressed and fed with breakfast on the table and lunch ready to go. This is a three-hour job in which time I get a lot done and accomplished for her. By 10 a.m. I'm running out the door back to Lynnwood and with 5 minutes to spare getting into the classroom where I teach Spanish to students second grade through 8th grade. A total of 75 students and certainly a challenge living in the 21st century, but I still like my job there. I'm there till 1:30 p.m. and then I come home for a one hour break and then I start my afternoon classes at home with my adult students doing private one on one lessons with them. By the time I'm done its 9 p.m. and time to cook dinner and do anything that I can fit into the remainder of my night. It's a very hectic schedule but I like it because it gives me the variety of working with all ages from seniors to children to in-between. I work very hard and I do my very best at each of my jobs.

Since I work hard I treat myself to my favorite dessert on Friday and on Saturday nights and that is ballroom dancing. I feel I am an accomplished dancer and I can swing and waltz and salsa as well as all the modern dances. Dancing has been my passion since I was 4 years old and I just enjoy the workout every weekend. I take my dancing as seriously as I do my work and I have a select number of dance partners that are always ready to match me on the dance floor.

Well, my husband thought that now since I had a limo that I could go dancing in style. (Actually he had other ideas, but we won't go there).

So here is the beginning of reality #1. Who was going to be my chauffeur??? And if I had one, was I going to PAY him??? With WHAT money??? I looked at this gorgeous car now sitting on my driveway as I parked it for the first time and thought about this. Who is going to drive me? Who knows how to drive a limo? WHO could I trust with such a car AND with my life???

I put an ad in a local paper for a chauffeur or someone worth training. This ad would run for couple of months as I checked out looser after looser. In the meantime, as I was starting to come out of my flu I started to think about starting my own limo business. I did not have the first clue as to what all it entailed but reality # 2 would soon hit me head on. I thought it would be as easy as getting a business license and insurance for the car. Oh reality of realities...

A business license. Hmmmmm. Try MANY business licenses!!! How about one for each city that you plan to do business in! Arrrgh! Each city having its own set of rules and fees.

Let me back up and say that there is no such thing as a place to go find out what ALL you need to be in business for a limo company. I would no sooner file one set of papers with one city only to find out that I had left something out or that their requirements were different. While I filed for the only license I thought I needed the master license with the State of Washington that was just the beginning. And there is nothing worst than calling up each city hall to get people who have worked there far too long so that they think YOU hearing their voice on the other line should be enough information for you, because they are clueless as to giving useful information. So you hang up and try again and after several efforts, I would find myself going there in person to see if I could get somewhere.

While I waited patiently for my master license to arrive (before finding out that I had a barrage of others to go get,) I started to have little things done to the car. Reality #3 sunk in. This limo needs major upgrades, if I'm going to try to get decent money for it as a for hire vehicle. And so it began... a trip to Car Toys (They treat me like royalty now). Let's see…replace, TV, VCR, Stereo, Phones, Intercom, add alarm system, add back up alarm system, add front PA system, check wiring and then the back breaker, the GPS system and computer which is a navigator system which will tell you step by step how to get from point A to point B. Did I tell you they really love me at Car Toys?

Then came the small details, inside accessories, glasses, napkins, cushions, steam cleaning of the inside, Oil changes, polish, etc.

Reality #4 just sat down...MONEY. With all the changes and upgrades and repairs I had made, I had just spent $10,000.00

In the meantime, the calls kept coming in from jerks and losers who did not have the first clue of being chauffeurs. They were too busy trying to live out their own fantasies while I was trying to get out the reality of my own.

So I thought, ok…now the car is ready, all I need is the master license and I'm off. Yeah right! Well in the meantime, I'll just order personalized plates. This was a good part of my fantasy, having a limousine with personal plates that read CARMEN1. I may not have a chauffeur but I had personalized plates! So off the order went.

I got the notice from the State that told me that in order to get my master license that I needed to go through an inspection with the limo and they sent a phone number to call for an appointment. I thought this would be a mechanical inspection and since I had the car's oils checked and it was running well that this would be no problem. So I called and made the appointment with the D.O.T. (Department of Transportation) and they gave me a date and time to be there and that was all.

I was so shocked when the inspection began, to out that this was not so much a mechanical inspection as it was a TOTAL inspection. But I had nothing to fear; after all I had just done $10,000 worth of improvements on the car.

The inspector was a lady, she was nice and friendly and she stood there in the pouring rain as I sat comfortably inside the driver's seat of the limo. She had her clip board with her and she walked this way and that around the car and then got in the back of the limo and sat there checking this and that out. Then she asked me to open the hood and show her where different things were.

She was writing things down with furiousness. Check...check...check...

Finally it was over and boy did I get the scolding of my life, or so it felt. I was told that the next time I brought the limo in better be in perfect condition otherwise I was just wasting hers and my time! She went over the list with me. She wrote me up on the two small cracks on the vinyl in the rear doors, the headliner edges were frayed, the windshield wipers washer were not working properly and the lights were not working!

Reality #5 I failed the inspection. I got home just in time to find the slap on my face...My personalized plates for CARMEN1 had arrived.

Reality #6 MORE money. More repairs. First I had to hunt for someone that could do the vinyl repairs and now I also had to fix the arm under the front driver's side because it was making a clunking sound. Oh heck, what's another thousand dollars!

The bad part about this whole thing is that as I made more made more repairs to the car I kept the bills from my dear husband and looked for ways to pay them on my own. I ended up getting my self into trouble with my own credit cards.

In the process of getting all the repairs done I was angry with the powers that be, that no one gave me any kind of papers to know what I should be prepared for in the inspection. No guidelines or anything. Just a notice that says you must go for an inspection. Well I learned that lesson the hard way. I had no clue what to expect but now I would know for the future.

Once again I went for the inspection and this time I sat in the vehicle for what seemed like an eternity as not one but two inspectors combed the car and every nook and cranny, writing things down. Watching them, I thought to myself, I'm cooked; I'm really cooked, what else could be wrong now?

Finally, they came around to me and this time the man spoke to me. He said "I could fail you right now for these minor things but seeing as how much effort and money you put into repairing the things from the last inspection then

I'll pass you this time but you have to fix the following things."

Well, those "following things" turned out to be getting a tiny bottle of white paint with the nail type brush and going over every tiny little nick outside the car. He told me that limo has to be in as perfect condition as possible since people are paying good money for it. Well, I could understand that, but after all the car was a 1989. Even so, that did not matter. Perfect means perfect she had said previously. BUT...I passed! What a relief!!!

I went home to celebrate and to send a copy of the inspection to Olympia for my master license. And of course it was not until AFTER I got the master license that I discovered that I needed to have a license from EACH city that I planned to do my business in. Oh brother!

We were getting close to the Christmas holidays and this being 1999 and all the hype about the Millennium and Y2K and party like it's 1999, well I was already counting my bank account to start growing beginning with the New Years Eve celebrations...even though I did not officially have any drivers!

The DJ at the dance club that I frequented agreed to do some promotional announcements for me during the 3 weeks preceding the New Years 1999 and in exchange I would give him 3 free hours of limo time. I figured this would be a small price to pay in exchange for all the calls that I was going to be getting during the holidays and New Years celebrations. I got zero calls. Deep in my heart I wished he'd forget that I'd made him the offer.

Well, I had given up on ever finding a personal chauffeur. In the course of waiting for the paperwork with the master license to go through, I had found one person who would qualify for a personal chauffeur, but it was short lived as I could not pay him and he did not have time for me anyway. Did I just say he qualified? How!?!?

I went on to place ads now for employ- ees. I thought if I could find 2 regulars and one back up that would work well So I place ads in various papers and once again I got calls from people who must really live in the twilight zone most of the time. It was discouraging to say the least.

The first city I applied to for a city license was my own city. I sent them the check and the application only to get it all back with a bunch of things circled. This was a joke. They were not satisfied with the $125.00 fee. They wanted to have my life story, account numbers, information about any stocks and bonds, and a copy of the deed to our house and mirage of other important documents, including a financial statement. For heaven's sake, all I wanted was a license.

My husband and I mulled over this again and again and we made the decision that we did not feel it was right or fair that we should have to produce information to the city that had no relevancy to my doing business by picking up or drop off a client. It was disappointing but I would not be able to do business in my own city. To drop off someone would be OK but I would not be allowed to pick up anyone in the city limits.

As I started to send off the other applications for other cities, I found that only my city did this. The others had a reasonable fee and soon the various city licenses were rolling in.

I started working on my business cards and brochures and also at the production of a web page. This would start off as another headache since once I enrolled into a program and gave them my credit card number all human forms of life would disappear and this thing called technical support would turn into endless hours of waiting for a mechanical operator which would in turn tell you to press 1 for this or 2 for that, etc. I ended up canceling out of one company and hooking up to another only to wait there was well and then make menacing calls to them because I could not figure out how to get my web page up.

I also signed up for my first point of advertisement. It sounded reasonable and was something I had not tried before in my past business ventures, so I would try it. They would cover 10,000 homes in my area. Unfortunately, the first batch of 10,000 coupons went out before I realized that I would not be doing business in my city, but fortunately, the 3 calls that I got from the coupons were located in the county.

In the meantime, two potentially good candidates had come about for limousine chauffeur. The first, a French man who I'll call Jack and he came for his interview impeccably dressed and ready to work. I was impressed by his demeanor and so I had my first chauffeur. The second was a woman who I'll call Penny. She was calling to inquire about the other possible positions in the company but she also expressed her interest as a chauffeur and she came across as a very warm and caring person, I agreed to interview with her as well. She turned out to be just fine. A third person called and he too fit the bill upon interviewing him. I'll call him George.

With the coupons now out; the phone was staring to ring and I needed to get my chauffeurs trained. I figured this would be a two-day training period. I had gotten an excellent lead on a man who is very well known in the Military and who has dined with several presidents. I had spoken to him back in late November when I first got the car and he had agreed to help me train my chauffeurs for a modest (really modest) fee. Meeting him was one of the best things that happened to me in my limo business. I'll call him John. His insight and professional manner and yet soft-spoken way were very structural in helping all of us.

So I called John and set up time and dates for our training sessions, which would be at the Embassy Suites Hotel in Board Room B.

The chauffeurs were instructed to be in uniform and both days would be filled with instruction from both John and myself and a couple of videos to watch as well as hands on training behind the wheel.

The dates were set for in two weeks and I got my employee manuals put together and lined up everything that we would need for this seminar.

While I waited for the two weeks to pass I went to the airport to get my certificate which allows me to be at the airport. If you don't have clearance with the airport ground transportation system you can't just hang around there with your limo I showed them my papers and they asked me for a paper which I was missing. I told them I had everything that Olympia had sent me, so the person handling the application walked to the car with me and checked in the glove compartment but still no papers, and furthermore he said there was a decal missing that was supposed to be on the back of the car but was not. So I would have to drive to Olympia to get this document that was still missing if I was to get that all important certificate for permission to the airport.

The next day I got up at 5 a.m. and got in my limo and drove all the way to Olympia, the state capital and requested the papers that were missing. "Oh you did not get them? They should have been sent to you with your master application. Sorry you had to come all the way here to get them!" Arrrgh!

I was in and out of there in 5 minutes and now I headed back to the airport. Once I got there, they accepted my application, but I would have to wait 48 hours for it to be processed and so I would have to come back again to get my photo taken after the processing would be done. So in a couple of days I was back at the airport again to get the ID badge with photo. I would have to work this into the training so that my chauffeurs would know where to go to get their badges done and also to show them where to park when they were at the airport.

Finally it looked like we were getting someplace with the mountain of paper-

work and forms and licenses and per-
mits.

Chapter Two

The day arrived for our training semi-nar. Day one would be two of the three chauffeurs and I, since Penny had an-other work commitment. Day two would be all three chauffeurs, and John and myself.

Jack arrived before the time and so he drank coffee that had been brought in while I got ready to give my presenta-tion. We waited for George...and we waited and we waited and we WAITED. Half an hour passed and I said enough is enough. I called him on my cell phone and a woman answered the phone. She sounded zonked and had no clue where he was. Well, where ever he was, he was not ever going to be in my good graces again for not calling to cancel. It was at that moment I learned Reality #7…get a deposit from prospective employees when planning a seminar. He ended up costing me money as a result of his non-appearance, breakfast, lunch, cap and badge. I was NOT happy. We continued on with our seminar just Jack and I and we accomplished a lot, as well as the trip to the airport for the submissions of his badge application. He would pick up his photo later that week.

Day number two of our seminar proved very fruitful as we added Penny and John to the meeting. We all learned a lot that day. The driver training provided by John was most helpful.

With the training finished we were now ready to roll wheels. Penny would come over to finish her training for day one during the following week and we too went to the airport to get her papers submitted. She would also have to return for her photo.

And now the fun begins...I'm not sure if you will need your crying rag or a calmant to help you settle down from laughing so hard.

Before the training period began I already had two runs scheduled. One was a round trip airport run and another a concert. I gave the concert to Jack and the airport run to Penny.

I got a 3rd call for a party of 6 for the same day that Penny and I were scheduled to go to the airport to do her badge paperwork and also to teach her how to use the navigational system, phone, etc. So I gave that run to Penny as well.

We left to the airport as soon as she arrived and in my mind she would be getting her badge today since the paperwork had already been sent ahead of time and so it should be there waiting for us, right? Wrong! They could not find the paperwork, so we got no where. The only good thing that came from the trip to the airport was that now she would know where to park the limo and what the steps would be each time she arrived to pick up a client or drop them off. I walked through the steps with her and instructed her to take the pink slip back to the car and put it in the front window on the inside... and don't forget to lock the car.

So she came back and off we went to take care of the application process. Well all this took longer than we expected since they could not find the paperwork, so we were gone some time. I would say about 40 minutes.

As we walked back out the doors to the line up of limousines I saw something white standing up that looked like a hood. I walked a little faster and faster still, when I realized that the rear hood of my limo was open, and wide open for all the other limo drivers to see and help themselves to all my supplies, etc., right there. "Penny" I said "oh no!"

The trunk has been open all this time. When you pressed the button on the remote to lock the door you must have pressed the trunk release instead!" Poor Penny was so embarrassed but we were both relieved to see that nothing had been taken or disturbed. We were so lucky too that it had not started to rain or everything would have been soaked.

We jumped back on the freeway and flew home to gas up and stock the inside coolers with refreshments for the night. On the way home I showed her how to use the navigation system which I was still having problems with myself, since I had little time to play with it. I also showed her how to use the cell phone and make calls and get calls. The car was now officially ready for its first run and after Penny ate something and refreshed her hair and makeup, she was ready. I was ready and CARMEN1 was ready.

Chapter Three

The First Run or how I ate my nails to the nubs…..

I had done all I could do with Penny and Jack and now it was time to let it all happen. I watched Penny drive off with my beautiful car and sent another prayer on behind her. I knew she could drive it. The rest would be common sense and trial and error. Hopefully less trial and error.

Penny called me after she dropped off the clients to their destinations. They had decided not to stick together and so half of the passengers went to one restaurant and the other half to another. Penny followed through with her instructions giving them each a card and asking them to call the cell number on the card for CARMEN1 when they were ready to depart.

We talked for a little while and she said everything was running smoothly. I was both grateful and happy. I saw my dollars waving to me from the bank.

And then Reality #8 happened.....

Another hour and a half passed and then the phone rang again. It was one of the men of the party. He was calling me to say that he was ready to be picked up I told him that the limo would be around momentarily and we hung up. Immediately I called Penny to the limo phone to let her know that this half of the party was ready. OH NO!!! After a couple of rings I got a prerecorded message saying the party that I was dialing had either turned off the phone or was out of the calling area!!! Oh NOOOOOOO! My first thought was that after Penny and I finished speaking that she pressed the wrong button and turned off the phone totally. Now there was absolutely NO WAY for me to communicate to her that these clients were ready! She herself had told me that she had given them business cards with the number of the limo phone on them No wonder they called me. They must have called and not been able to get through and so now they were calling me….but it was no use. I sat there in just about a cold sweat and almost in tears, while my husband watched me moaning and groaning as if I'd broken every bone in my body. I was soooooo cooked. He suggested some lame brain ideas like let's call a taxi to drive around looking for a limo sitting there....there WHERE??? The half of the party that called me was not the half I had written on my contract. I knew one of the restaurants but since they had a change of plans at the last moment I did not know the name to the second place. Only Penny knew that and she might as well be in outer space. I could now see myself writing a refund check for this night and my dollars marching back out from my account waving to me as they left. I realized too now that if they were ready to be picked up that the other side must have already called her and gotten no response either and so now I had two parties and a limo and a chauffeur and NO WAY to get to any of them!

I kept hitting the redial key to the limo phone over and over and kept getting the same message. Then I realized that I could hit the *69 key on my phone and get the last number that called me…the waiting client! I tried the limo phone one more time before calling the client.

This time she answered. "PENNY" I screamed. She was totally unaware of what was taking place and I told her I'd explain later for now to go quickly and pick up the second half of the party because they were waiting. I sat back in thankful prayer! My dollars were now doing an about face and heading back to the bank.

That night when Penny came back with the limo, I explained it all to her and she tried to figure out what she had done different that would cause the phone not to ring. This all happened in the time frame that she shut the car off. Apparently the phone shuts down too. We both looked more closely at this cell phone and we both discovered that it was quite a difficult phone to operate. I knew that I never wanted to find myself in this predicament again so the first thing I did the next day was to change the phone and service to Nextel, which is a much easier phone to use but the added bonus that it has a walkie talkie built right in so communication is instantaneous. We can talk by regular cell means or by walkie-talkie means and this would work, perfect for us.

The first kink had been taken care of after so many upgrades and repairs. After that first run, the car came back and went through a complete inside vacuum and clean up and restocking. Our next run would be in a week for an airport run for a mother and her two daughters that had never been in a limo. It would be a morning run so we would provide hot coffee and croissants and a little gift to each of the ladies.

I got all the necessary paperwork ready for Penny on her clipboard and input the clients address into the navigational address book so that it would be ready to call up. Out of my own curiosity I decided to check and see how well the navigational program worked since I still had not seen it work to its full potential. For the thousands that I paid, I really was not impressed and I felt like I had over paid because of this. So I hit the proceed button and waited for the instructions to take me to the clients house. Nothing. I drove to the end of the block and tried again. Nothing. I drove a little closer to her house. Still nothing. FINALLY, I was a block away from Car Toys where I bought it and I called in to the store and requested the manager to come out and help me. By this time I was really upset because I had yet to see the navigator work and stay working after I would turn it off. It's like it kept going back to a default point. They agreed to fix it and have it ready by the next run.

Well, they fixed it and it went down again By now I was starting to lose my happy face They told me that it was not the Navigator system that had the problem but that there was a problem in the electrical system that was caus-ing a shortage of amps and as the am-page got low then it caused the memory to get lost putting me back to square one. Suddenly, I was looking at another pool of repairs. It would mean that I would have to find an electrician that works on limousines and have all the electrical tested to find the problem. I don't even want to know what they would charge. I knew it would not be cheap I started to look around for an electrician but my heart was not in the search. Tomorrow I would have an airport run and I would have to send off Penny with just written directions to the clients' house. Having this $7,000.00 gizmo in my car that did nothing was really making me upset now. The car was running fine otherwise. Now did I want to go and see what was the problem with the electrical or did I want to take the GPs system back and demand a refund credit and if I did would I get it. I guess I would soon find out.

The morning of the airport run came and you'd think that I was taking the President of the United States to the airport. Hot coffee, sweet rolls, petite fleurs and orange juice for a party of 3 ordinary ladies. WHY do I do this??? WHY am I like this??? Why can't I be like those other people out there who do things only half way! That would be nice. Why do I have to be one of those that dots every i and crosses every t. Service with a smile, give them the shirt off your back and your wallet and bank account as well. WHY WHY WHY??? What a horrible sickness to always make sure everything is done right. I really and truly am beginning to understand why God has kept me without a business for all my life, because every time I have a business I do too much and give too much and lose too much. It was this way with the wedding business as a wedding consultant and in a year's time, I fitted myself into a $27,000 debt. Here I am again in the same boat, lots of input and $$$ from my end and no business to show for it. My stomach hurts.

After I figured my cost and the salary for the day I had come out negative $30.00 I sat at my desk holding my head and wondering how and when does it turn around for me so that I can make money instead of only putting out money.

Chapter Four

I had gotten another phone call from the party that we did with the drunks and now he wanted an airport run plus a return run. Already I was not looking forward to that. This would be my last run since I decided there was just no money to be made there.

In the meantime, I got an email from the 2nd person who signed with us for the concert. She was mad because, I had charged the bill on her credit card in full. Well what was I supposed to do? After reading her nasty note, I wrote back to her with all the calm and professionalism one can send through the Internet and explained to her that she had given me the authority to bill her account at the time the card numbers were given. Of course now she wanted me to cancel it and start all over again and change the hours, etc. I was not about to credit her account at this time. Heck, I'd just sent off my limo insurance premium with that money in the bank. There was NO money to credit back to her account. If she got belligerent I would have to borrow from my husband to pay it and cancel her out totally. I waited from her to reply and hoped that the soft answer I sent her would satisfy her and we could get on with the concert date as planned.

Still sitting here thinking about the electrical problem and what to do about it, the phone rang. It was Penny and before she even spoke I could tell what her conversation would be about as I sensed it in her voice and her tone. She needed a job with more hours and I could not give her that, yet. I was trying to be encouraging but how do you do that when you are realizing that instead of going forward you are going backward. How did I get myself into this mess? I could not blame her for feeling that she needed out and if I'd been in the same position I would have felt the same too, so now all I could hope for was that Jack would not bail on me or I'd be doomed for good. The ads continued to run for personal chauffeur as well and I continued to get calls from shmucks. How pathetic could it get. I had a great limo with dwindling workers and I could not even find someone to be a personal chauffeur in exchange for free room and board!

A few days later, I got an email from the concert lady again. Before even opening her email I Hoped that she was not upset and that she would see things my way and we could go on from there...but I was wrong.

She demanded her account be credited and said she had never authorized me to charge her account...even though she gave me her credit card number. Her letter was strong and forceful and at this point I thought, why would I even want someone like this in MY LI-MO. I sent her a reply telling her that I would credit her account but not without getting the last word in with a few choice words of my own.

I sat at my table and looked at my check register as the numbers got less and less. I thought the idea was that the numbers were supposed to get bigger. I thought I must be the first limousine company ever that does not make money but gives it away. Oh. My stomach hurts.

I had written a letter to the party with the phone incident to apologize for any inconvenience and I got a call from the man who assured me that it was OK and that he appreciated my even writing to him. So he booked an airport run, which I, like a hungry dog took like crumbs off the table. But this would be my last airport run. After having done the first one having realized that instead of making any money I came up negative $30.00 there would be NO more airport runs after this one as a courtesy to the man.

It was Saturday night and I was working hard to push all thoughts of the limo business out of my head. What a week it had been. One negative after another. I had just credited the account for the concert lady and the whole thing was settling over me like a dark cloud.

The phone ran and Mrs. P. called. The lady from the first airport run. When I heard her name over the phone I held my breath and waited for more bad news. But she was very nice and in fact very happy and she was calling me from Hawaii to say what a wonderful service we provided for her and what a wonderful chauffeur Penny was and all that. She couldn't say enough about the service. Having been just chewed up on the other end with the other lady, it was a little difficult for me to hold my chin up. I thought to myself if she only knew that Penny had decided to leave and I myself would be the one picking her up; but I said nothing and told her I was so happy things went well for her. Her words were encouraging, but since I was not going to do any more airport runs after the next scheduled one and I would not have Penny, well, like I said; it was hard to get excited.

Tonight I was going to dance till I had nothing but nubs left for feet, so I dressed in one of my "dance all night" dresses and off I went in my baby blue Cadillac. My first stop was to the gas station to get gas and as I drove in the driveway I saw a white limo just like mine pulling out just ahead of me. I watched it as it drove away gracefully and into the night. I sighed thinking to myself that could be me. I stopped and picked up my girlfriend on the way and we chatted all the way to the club. Once we got situated and after a few minutes the DJ walked in and greeted us. He said to me "...by the way...when you have a moment...." Oh no! Here it came...pay up time. What else! I got ZERO calls for the car during the holidays but I had to live up to my end of the deal since he had plugged the limo for me during the holiday dances. "I'd like to use my 3 free hours next week for my girlfriend's b-day" Those words seemed to fall on my ears like unadulterated lead. Not only had I had to give money back today, now I was being further reduced to being my own chauffeur. There was no point to say anything. A deal was a deal, and so I meekly accepted the directions and said "I'll be there."

I slumped into my chair. My evening was finished before I got a chance to start. Gloria looked at me and said "…honey, I'll ride with you. You got an extra cap I can wear?" After some thought, I decided that I would just take a change of clothes with me and since they would end up in the same disco anyway, he did not want a return trip home, then I could just park my limo, change clothes and then go in for dancing and then take Gloria home after that and be on my way.

Chapter Five

It was Sunday and time for Jack to do that second airport run. He came on schedule and I was happy to see him. I was not sure how I'd tell him that the concert run had been canceled, he was so cheerful. And then I learned why. Jack explained to me that he was now also working for another Limousine Company and getting lots of runs from them. He let me know that he was still available for me but in the meantime he needed work and money too and so what could I say. I instructed him in his log for the day and his route feeling now somewhat intimidated. 2 weeks ago this man knew nothing about the limousine business and today he was working for another limousine company with the FREE training that I had given him. I handed over the keys and he saluted me as he drove off. I stepped back and watched CARMEN1 leave.

I knew where I would be next weekend, enjoying my limousine…as a driver. My husband asked me if we were going to get to enjoy the limousine for our upcoming anniversary the following week. "Yeah sure" I said. I'll drive you one way and you can drive me the other."

The return trip to the airport for Jack's recent trip was scheduled and ready to go. Jack came and picked up the car and off he went. The client was to meet him at the baggage door upon his arrival. 15 minutes came and went...half an hour...45 minutes, no client. Jack called me on the walkie-talkie for assist as to what to do. We decided to call and leave a message for the client at his home letting him know that we had waited for him and he was a no show.

In the mean time, I got another call from Hawaii from Mrs. P. She had changed her return flight time and would be coming back at her original time. Since Penny was no longer available, I would have to see if Jack could do it and since the limo was already at the airport and he only lived 5 minutes away from the airport then it would be better if he could just keep the limo. Go home and then do the run in the morning right from where he was. That would save me a few bucks.

Jack went back to the limo once we decided that the client he was waiting for was not going to show. In a few minutes the walkie-talkie beeped again.

"Carmen... you got a ticket on the

Limousine!
Oh please! Somebody just bury me already! A ticket was placed on the limo because Penny had removed the permit sign from the window and placed it in the glove compartment. It was to remain in plain sight on the window while at the airport. I could see myself pleading now "...Please. Mr. Judgeship... don't give me this ticket! My nin-cum-poop chauffeur in training stuck it in the

glove compartment and forgot to take it out. Pleazzzzze your highness!"

This had been a long day. I took a hot shower and went to bed, totally defeated.

The next day, I ran home after job #2 and took the limo to an electrical place that works on cars and those kinds of problems. I explained to them that I was having problems with the navigator system and that it kept going back to default because there was not enough amperage to hold the memory. They charge $65.00 an hour. Well, either I find out once and for all if there is an electrical problem there or not so that I an find out if I should keep the navigation device or take it back and demand my $6,000.00 They would call me when the check with the car was over and any repairs made.

I got home to a call from the man who missed his flight and did not show the day before. I had called to leave him a message that we were there. Where was he?

He must have picked up his messages because now he was calling me back...

mad at ME, because he said he told ME that he was coming back on Thursday, not Tuesday. I looked on my contract and on my calendar and clearly it was marked for Tuesday and not Thursday. Thinking to myself that I just did not want to deal with another jerk this week, I said fine and told him a chauffeur would be there to pick him up. What he did not know was that it would not be Jack or my limo.

Since I was going to lose money on this run it did not matter if I was paying my chauffeur or some outsider and since my limo would not be ready anyway, I had NO car.

I did the unthinkable and called another chauffeur from another limo company whom I'd swore I would never call, especially since he stood me up 3 times in the past. But at this point I was going to lose money no matter which route I took... I might as well put my worst customer with the worst chauffeur I could find and hope that they would find each other.

I called Danny and gave him the job order. He accepted and apologized that he had stood me up. He also told me that he was looking forward to meeting me. "Look" I told him. " I don't care if I ever meet you. I don't even want to meet you. I just want you to pick up this client from the airport and take him home and come and get your money. Period."

My next call this day came from Mrs. P. she wanted to thank me for the splendid service. Considering all the muck I was muddling in, this little stroke of positive was like a piece of bread being thrown to a beggar.

A call came in for a limo run. A party of 8 girls and it was a sweet 16 occasion. I took the order and called Jack to let him know I would need him for Saturday. Oh well!!!....now suddenly I was no longer Jack's priority...me...the one who TRAINED HIM! His calendar was full of runs he had to make for this other company. I sat back and felt like the tears would just burst forth any moment. I really felt betrayed. I marked my calendar for Saturday. I, myself would be doing the run.

Still one more call for me this night. The man who was interested in the live-in chauffeur position for personal chauffeur called. He apologized for having to miss his appointment last week and asked for another appointment convenient for him. At this point, I lit into him like a bee that just got stung, and only until I was out of words did I get quiet. I agreed to meet him one last time and I warned him of certain death should he cancel out one more time.

Chapter Six

The sweet 16 party came and went without a hitch. I did the run myself and the girls enjoyed themselves and opened their gifts and played their music on the way to the Seattle Center. I had called my friend Gloria to let her know that I would not be able to go out with her that night because of my run, but she volunteered to go with me and keep me company for this first time event for me. We had a good time in the front while the party was going on in the back and I was grateful to my friend for her going with me.

The chauffeur wannabe never showed and I made sure to note that there would be no further communication between us. I'd had enough. I put a new ad in the newspaper to advertise for a chauffeur but this time I also wanted someone who could be a gardener by day and chauffeur by night. The weeks would pass again before I would meet the appropriate person for the job.

A call came in from an acquaintance that I know from the place I go dancing to. The man, who called for a limo, was someone that I thought was very high end and a highly intelligent business man. I had danced with him many times before this call came in.

He explained to me that he wanted to hire the limo for about 7 hours and that he wanted to impress some work associates or clients and he wanted to show them a good time.

I called Jack and he was not available. (Why did I think he would be?) And so I planned the run for myself. I came home from a full day or work on Friday and showered and prepared the limousine for its night out.

I arrived on time to the client/ "friend" who lives in Kirkland and then from there we went to Kent to pick up the other guests which consisted of 1 man and 7 women which brought it to a full car with 9 passengers.

I carefully filled the limo bar with ice and soft drinks in the wall and CARMEN 1 was spotless clean. When the client got in he raved about what a gorgeous car it was and how he'd not been in such a nice limousine before.

We arrived to Kent and then the act du circus began. The other 7 women piled into the car. The client had brought with him a large cooler of assorted booze which he took into the limousine with him He asked me if he could replace my soda with his booze and I said fine.

The limo had not moved from its stationary position before the first drinks were poured by the client for all his passenger guests. These were not just drinks; these were mammoth drinks in 18 oz. glasses.

The first round of drinks had not even finished when one of my expensive gold filigree glasses broke. The limousine had not even begun to move. I had not even shut the door, before the first glass broke. The client removed all the glasses and passed them to me asking me if I could put them away in the trunk.

I hid my hurt as best as possible. I'd had these glasses for so long given to me by someone who was very near and dear to me at one point in my life and I had chosen to give my best this night and now one of the "pre-drunks" had broken it without so much as an I'm sorry. I said nothing and put the broken glass in the trunk with the sodas that I'd just gotten done removing as well.

I slipped into the driver's seat and off I went with my limousine full.

They had a large cooler full of assorted hard liquor but I was instructed to stop at different bars in Seattle where they would get off to go in and drink more.

With each successive stop they came out more and more and more drunk. Their behavior as responsible adults went out the window together with their underwear, socks and who knows what else they threw out. I believe I went to about 5 different places. By the time I reached the 5th place they were all in the twilight zone.

I opened the door to let them know we'd arrived and what a sight they were to behold. Totally disheveled, half naked, some sleeping on top of others and a couple in particular looking like they would vomit any moment. The limousine reeked of alcohol and any re-spect I had for this client went out the window to ground zero.

"We've arrived" I summoned. One of them managed to open their eyes.

"Oh never mind...just take us back to Kent..."

Did I mention that this entire evening it had been raining heavily? This rain made it so difficult to see the signs and road well, and by now it was past 2 in the morning.

I made the trek back to Kent and all was silent in the back...for a short while. About 25 minutes later, I began to hear laughter in the back and now the passengers began together with their drunkenness to become vulgar. I heard such things as "...go ahead just touch it." One man said to a woman " ...I'll give you $100.00 if you'll just kiss it." And while he tempted the women the others there laughed.

Even though I had the glass partition up, but they were being so loud and yelling at each other like deaf people that it was easy to hear what was being said in the back even though I would have preferred not to.

By the time we reached Kent, they had finished every last bottle of liquor they had. When I opened the passenger door, one of the 2 men stepped out first. I've never seen such a pathetic sight of women to follow. Actually, they could not follow. They could not even sit up. The first woman came out of the limo...hands first, feet last, literally crawling out. The next woman kept refusing to come out of the limousine, while one was busy using my brand new ice bucket to vomit in. Another woman was asleep and still another was complaining that she could not remember where she lived. I've never seen such a sorry sight. No one could find their car keys and when they did, they could not remember what kind of car they had! And there was the client as plastered as the rest of them, still in the limousine making out with one of the other women and looking like they would go at it any moment....and they did on the floor of the office they came from, they finally got out of the limo, right inside the big glass window that people would normally pass by on the street.

This party of people was so drunk that the other man told me he would not let them attempt to drive their own cars home, so between he and I, we would have to drive them home. He would direct me where to go and in this manner we would get each woman home. First, we would have to figure out how to find the right houses, since they all forgot their addresses and could not tell us where to go had their life depended on it. So here I am driving up one road and down another looking for what might be a suitable house for them, till they'd recognize their house and I would stop.

In the meantime the client was getting it on in the front window of the office where we left him and one of his bimbos. When we got back to that office; the man who'd been with me taking the others home went in and I could see from the outside that he was reprimanding his buddy for not going in a back room and doing his thing in public for all the world to see...except that fortunately for all the world it was now 3 in the morning and most of the world sleeping in Kent.

It was time to take the client home and his male friend and his "toy" for the night back to Kirkland. It never stopped raining all night and before I drove off,

I had him sign the credit card slip and contract agreement and off I went. He paid for his event via credit card.

I got back to Lynnwood and stopped at the gas station to empty the car and assess the damage. I filled two large lawn sized bags with empty bottles of booze and large size plastic glasses. It was amazing how they could drink all that and still drink more at the bars they went to. Well that's all I did, I was too tired to do any more. In the morning I would check the rest of the limo out. I drove home, hit the shower and went to bed.

I got up at noon the next morning and then went back to the limousine to start the clean up. It was then that I noticed the puke in the ice buckets and also puke stains on two different areas of carpet. I was so upset that this was the same limousine that had been complimented on its grandeur and how badly they had treated the car with no respect or regard for someone else's property. I went back in the house and when I ran the credit charges through, I added an additional $100.00 charge for vomit clean up as stated in the contract. It took me 3 hours to totally restore the limousine to clean and fresh again and when I was done I went straight to my computer and changed my contract to read "clean up charge for vomit $200.00"

I never heard from the client again and I hope never to see him again.

Chapter Seven

Many weeks had gone by for the chauffeur position ad and finally I got a call from someone that I thought would be a good possibility or at least half good. Charlie. Mexican born...accent, clean, modest, and quiet. I interviewed him for about 2 hours and came to my conclusion that he would be a good candidate for the job. He'd lost his wife 6 months ago and was still in the grieving process, but he was trying to put his life back together and I thought that this would work well for both of us. He would be a gardener by day for a couple of hours a day and then I would use him to chauffeur for me on the weekends that the limo was not in use and I would train him to be a paid employee as well. So within a week he was moved in and we started with the yard work first as I worked my schedule around him to start training him for the chauffeuring part as well.

Within a week he'd found a "second job" to do as a milk deliveryman. He would be getting up at 3 in the morning to do this job and then his plan was that he would come home do yard work and chauffeur on the weekends and still have a life!

By the end of the third week I was mowing my own grass again and the yard work was not getting done. I was getting to the point with each passing day that I'd come home specifically looking to see what he'd done and nothing was done.

Now it was Friday and no yard work had been done all week. I'd made plans to go dancing with Gloria to check out a new club and this would be his first attempt at chauffeuring and she and I would be the guinea pigs. We were supposed to leave the house at 7 PM to pick her up.

I went downstairs to see if he was ready at 7 PM and found that he was not even dressed yet! He'd been sleeping and was still walking around in a fog. I went back to the limo and sat and wait and waited. 25 minutes later, he showed up ready. By the time we got to Gloria's house, we'd lost some time and then in trying to get out of her neighborhood, he got the scenic tour of all the neighbors' houses. This cost us another 15 minutes. We'd hoped to get to the new club by 8 so as to try out the free dance lessons and be there an hour before heading back to our regular club. But that was not the case.

By the time we finished with the neighborhood scenic tour we gave up on going to the other club and I told Charlie to just go straight to our usual club. I was having a hard time getting into my Friday groove. I was not happy with the way things were going with this guy and yet what could I do... I had no one else. And so the Friday went.

Saturday night, would be the first prom night for the limo and so I did not stay out late on Saturday night but came home early in time to make sure that Charlie was up and dressed and that the limousine was ready to go and leave on time for the prom.

I did not see Charlie again till Monday when he came to pick up his paycheck. I was already to fire him but I held back and tried with all my might to hold off and not lose my cool with him.

I brought up the fact that I felt I'd now been put on the back burner because of this milk delivery job, but he assured me that he was just learning the route and that it would not always be like this.

I went over the facts again and again but he insisted that he would get faster as he got more secure with what he was supposed to do. Hesitantly, I gave him his allowance for May plus the pay check for the last run.

Now suddenly the phone was starting to ring more and more for prom runs. We were in prom season and finally the phone was ringing for the limousine! We had proms booked for each Saturday in May.

I was still not satisfied with the speed with which Charlie was working at as gardener and his speed in learning as a chauffeur, but as each week would pass I would tell myself to remain calm and continue to look the other way with his slowness, hoping that his abilities would improve sooner than later and that we would get past the present hurdles.

It was now nearing the middle of May and it was time for another repair job... another major repair job...the air conditioning unit was kaput. Please do not pass go,...do not collect $200.00... This repair would cost $875.00 and when I was done with that, I would need to drive directly to the place where the alignments are done and be sure to pay the nice guys there another $100.00 for a badly needed alignment.

Ahhh, but now (seems I keep saying this)...the repairs were all done and there was nothing more to be done. And once again...I had a negative balance in my checking account.

May 16th... my 48th birthday and a date with the judge. I'm not sure if this would be a good thing or not but all I could do was to lay my cards before the judge and let him know that the mistake made by my chauffeur was truly a sincere and honest one...not to mention dumb.

I got to my appointment 2 hours early. Halfway hoping that I could just breeze in and out (only because it was my birthday). Actually, I did not say any-thing to anyone there about that. It re-mained my secret.

When 1 p.m. finally came, the secre-tary summoned me and said "They are ready for you." THEY? Who is THEY? I thought it was a HE. But instead it was THEY…and sure enough, THEY it was … all 5 of THEY. I mean them!

I was feeling quite dumb at this point but since I had already sent my letter ahead for appeal then there was not much more to be said. I was motioned to sit down before them on the opposite side of the table. They all sat in silence with their noses buried in a copy of my letter. One of them looked up quickly and told me that they were just reviewing the letter and then he too stuck his nose back into the paper.

After 5 minutes they all looked up in unison and looked me over. "Is there anything you want to add to this?" Asked one.

"No. I believe that I have stated my case clearly and except to repeat that I'm very sorry and this won't happen again. I am a new business and my chauffeur was doing his first run at the airport that day and was not aware or did not remember that the certificate needed to be on the window. It had been placed in the glove compartment by the other chauffeur."

They said nothing and looked at each other almost as if they were trying not to smile I sat there twitching my hands in my lap.

"Thank you. We will let you know via mail the decision."

And that was it. I left to go home. At least this was done and over. I tried my best and was honest with them. There was nothing else I could do.

Chapter Eight

I had just gotten my yellow page advertisement into print and into the Internet just in time for prom season. The calls started to come in and for the month of May I averaged one prom a week. They were all 4-hour deals, but I was glad to at least get my feet wet. It was nice to feel like I was finally doing something with my limo.

Four weeks passed and the decision came from the Port of Seattle for the citation. They waived the fine and let me go. Hooray!! I was so grateful not to have to pay this fine.

Now prom season was ended and I'd had a taste of what it was like. I found that it went pretty well and since I had strictly written into my contract agreement a stiff penalty for limousine abuse, it had gone well with me. Next year this time I would be a seasoned prom director for my limousine.

Next in line would be wedding season. This would be another interesting venture and I hoped as simple as doing proms, however I would ever get to do any weddings. In fact, the limo would never go out again after the last prom.

It was now the middle of May and things had not improved with Charlie one bit. It was Friday night and I was ready to go out for the night. Gloria was waiting for me to pick her up, but 7 p.m. came and went and Charlie never showed up. 7:30…8:00…8:30…and no Charlie.

"This is it!!! This is it!!! He is sooo Fired" I thought. I called Gloria to let her know that I'd pick her up myself but for the remainder of the night I thought about how I was going to carve Charlie into a tree when I got home.

Well, not only did he not come home on Friday night but neither did he show up for Saturday and for that matter he disappeared for an entire week. By the time his milk employer had called asking for his whereabouts and we had both called the police to file a missing persons report; I really began to get concerned about him because I knew in my heart how badly he missed his wife and I did feel sorry for him. That was the whole reason for my holding back from firing him sooner.

Finally a week passed and I finally found him. He had gone on a drinking binge with his buddies and disappeared to hide out till he was done. I was furious when I found this out because he had told me that he was a nondrinker. I gave him notice and he had 24 hours to come and get his belongings before I would put them out. I was so upset when he finally came that I did not even want to look at him. He left owing me money and in far worse condition that when he arrived. Although I did feel bad for him but I realized that this was the lot that he chose and he had the opportunity to make things better for himself if he really wanted to I also discovered that he smoked weed and this was the final straw for me. I could not feel sorry any longer. I was once again without a chauffeur.

I placed ads again for live in chauffeur/gardener but the calls that came in and the quality of the applicants left little to be desired and the ads were not cheap.

Since the time of the last prom not one call came in. The limo sat and sat and sat. The battery went dead a couple of times over and it sat some more.

I was getting buried under the cost of the monthly insurance fee and now the yellow page ads which I did not want in the first place but which my dear husband badgered me into, to the point that I did it to make him quiet. I wish now I'd resisted no matter what because now I had to pay monthly for a year.

The day came when I could not keep up with the expenses and no money coming in to cover for the insurance or ads.

I approached my husband and laid it on the line. I offered to give the limo back to him since I could not pay for those costs any more. I would live with the final outcome.

He told me that he had gotten me the limo in the first place for pleasure and not for business and after much thought he said it would be best to close down the business aspect of it and just keep the limo for what it was originally intended...pleasure.

The next day I called the insurance company and canceled out the insurance. The agent told me I was getting out at a good time since she said insurance rates would double for cars for hire in the next year. We would certainly hear about it in the news. I called the various places and canceled out everything that needed to be canceled associated to the limo, but I would still have to pay for those wretched phone book ads that I was so much against placing in the first place. There was no way out of that since the book was already out.

The last time that the limousine was used would be its most elegant date of all, for the wedding of my daughter and I confess, that was the best date of all.

THE END